UNLEASH THE POWER OF PERSUASIVE COPYWRITING:

Boost Your Fiverr Sales Today!

HENRY JONES

Copyright © 2023

by Henry Jones

TABLE OF CONTENTS

INTRODUCTION

In today's digital age, persuasive copywriting is more important than ever. With the sheer volume of content being produced and consumed every day, standing out and capturing the attention of potential customers is crucial. Whether you're selling a product or service, or simply trying to build an audience, persuasive copywriting is the key to success.

However, it's not just about getting noticed - it's about getting results. Persuasive copywriting is about using language, psychology, and storytelling to influence and persuade your audience to take action. This could be anything from purchasing to signing up for a newsletter or sharing your content with others.

In this book, you'll learn the art and science of persuasive copywriting, and how to apply it to your Fiverr gigs. You'll discover how to use proven persuasion techniques to write headlines that grab attention, craft compelling body copy, and optimize your gigs for maximum results. With the help of real-life case studies and examples, you'll see how these strategies can be applied to your own copywriting, and start seeing the results for yourself.

So, if you're ready to take your Fiverr sales to the next level, this book is for you. Whether you're a seasoned pro or just starting, you'll find the insights, techniques and strategies you need to create persuasive and effective copy that drives results.

Overview of the Book's Content and Goals

In this book, we will delve into the intricacies of understanding persuasion. Persuasion is the art of convincing someone to take a particular course of action, and it is the foundation of persuasive copywriting. Understanding how persuasion works is essential for creating effective copy that drives results.

We will begin by exploring the psychology of persuasion. You'll learn about the various cognitive biases and heuristics that influence our decision-making, and how to use them to your advantage. From there, we will delve into the most common persuasion techniques and how to use them effectively.

Next, we'll explore the role of storytelling in persuasion. Storytelling is a powerful tool that can be used to capture attention, build emotional connections, and drive action. You'll learn how to craft compelling stories that align with your message, and how to use them to persuade your audience.

Once you have a solid understanding of persuasion, we'll move on to the next step: crafting compelling copy. You'll learn how to write headlines that grab attention, craft persuasive body copy, and use language to influence and persuade. We'll also cover strategies for creating effective Fiverr gig descriptions and tips for using Fiverr's platform to your advantage.

To further illustrate these concepts and strategies, we'll include several case studies and examples of successful Fiverr gigs. You'll see the copywriting techniques used in these examples, and learn how to apply them to your gigs.

In conclusion, this book is designed to give you a comprehensive understanding of persuasion, and how to apply it to your own copywriting. Whether you're a seasoned pro or just starting, you'll find the insights, techniques, and strategies you need to create persuasive and effective copy that drives results. With the help of this book, you'll be able to unleash the power of persuasive copywriting and boost your Fiverr sales today.

UNDERSTANDING PERSUASION

The Psychology of Persuasion

In this section of the book, we will focus on understanding persuasion and how it can be used to create effective copy. Persuasion is the art of convincing someone to take a particular course of action, and it is the foundation of persuasive copywriting. Understanding how persuasion works is essential for creating copy that drives results.

First, let's explore the psychology of persuasion. When it comes to persuasion, it's important to understand the various cognitive biases and heuristics that influence our decision-making. These cognitive biases are mental shortcuts that our brains use to make sense of the world around us. For example, the "anchoring effect" is a cognitive bias where the first piece of information presented, such as a price, sets the standard for subsequent decisions. By understanding these cognitive biases, you can use them to your advantage in your copywriting.

Next, let's talk about the most common persuasion techniques. Some of the most effective persuasion techniques include social proof, authority, scarcity, and reciprocity. Social proof, for example, is the idea that people will be more likely to take a particular action if they see that others are doing it. This can be used in copywriting by highlighting how many people have purchased a product or service, or by featuring testimonials from satisfied customers. Authority, on the other hand, is the idea that people are more likely to be persuaded by someone who is an expert in their field. This can be used in copywriting by highlighting the qualifications of the person or company behind the product or service. Scarcity is the idea that people are more likely to be persuaded by something that is in limited supply, while reciprocity is the idea that people are more likely to be persuaded by something that they feel they owe in return.

Another important aspect of persuasion is storytelling. Storytelling is a powerful tool that can be used to capture attention, build emotional connections, and drive action. By crafting compelling stories that align with your message, you can use them to persuade your audience. For example, a story about how a product helped a customer overcome a particular problem can be much more effective than a dry list of features and benefits.

Once you have a solid understanding of persuasion, the next step is to apply it to your copywriting. This includes writing headlines that grab attention, crafting persuasive body copy, and using language that influences and persuades. It is also important to optimize your copy for the platform it will be used on, in this case, Fiverr. This includes creating effective gig descriptions and using Fiverr's platform to your advantage.

To further illustrate these concepts and strategies, we will include several case studies and examples of successful Fiverr gigs throughout the book. These examples will show you the copywriting techniques used in real-life scenarios and how they can be applied to your gigs.

In conclusion, understanding persuasion is crucial for creating effective copy that drives results. By understanding the psychology of persuasion, the most common persuasion techniques, and the power of storytelling, you can apply these concepts to your own copywriting and see the results for yourself. This book is designed to give you a comprehensive understanding of persuasion and how to apply it to your own copywriting, specifically on Fiverr. With the help of this book, you'll be able to create persuasive and effective copy that drives results and boost your Fiverr sales.

Common Persuasion Techniques and How to Use Them Effectively

In this section of the book, we will be focusing on the common persuasion techniques and how to use them effectively in your copywriting. As we have discussed earlier, persuasion is the art of convincing someone to take a particular course of action, and it is the foundation of persuasive copywriting. Understanding and applying these persuasion techniques can make a significant difference in the effectiveness of your copy.

One of the most effective persuasion techniques is social proof. Social proof is the idea that people will be more likely to take a particular action if they see that others are doing it. This can be used in copywriting by highlighting how many people have purchased a product or service, or by featuring testimonials from satisfied customers. For example, if you are selling a product on Fiverr, highlighting the number of positive reviews or the number of purchases can increase the perceived value of the product, and make it more likely for someone to buy it.

Another persuasion technique is authority. Authority is the idea that people are more likely to be persuaded by someone who is an expert in their field. This can be used in copywriting by highlighting the qualifications of the person or company behind the product or service. For example, if you are a certified professional in a certain field, highlighting that in your gig description can increase the perceived value of your service and make you stand out from other gig providers.

Scarcity is another persuasion technique that can be effectively used in copywriting. Scarcity is the idea that people are more likely to be persuaded by something that is in limited supply. This can be used in copywriting by highlighting the limited availability of a product or service, or by creating a sense of urgency. For example, if you are selling a service on Fiverr, highlighting that you only have a limited number of spots available can create a sense of urgency, and make people more likely to buy your service.

Reciprocity is another persuasion technique that can be used effectively in copywriting. Reciprocity is the idea that people are more likely to be persuaded by something that they feel they owe in return. This can be used in copywriting by providing something of value for free, such as an e-book or a free consultation. For example, if you are selling a service on Fiverr, offering a free consultation can make people more likely to buy your service because they feel they owe you something in return.

Another persuasion technique that can be effectively used in copywriting is the use of emotional appeals. Emotions play a significant role in decision-making, and connecting with the emotions of your audience can make your message more effective. By evoking emotions such as happiness, excitement, or fear, you can create a strong emotional connection with your audience and make them more likely to take action.

Another technique is the use of storytelling. Storytelling is a powerful tool that can be used to capture attention, build emotional connections, and drive action. By crafting compelling stories that align with your message, you can use them to persuade your audience. For example, a story about how a product helped a customer overcome a particular problem can be much more effective than a dry list of features and benefits.

The use of rhetorical devices such as rhetorical questions, repetition, and rhetorical triangles can also be effective in persuasion. Rhetorical questions can be used to encourage thought and introspection. Repetition can be used to emphasize a point and make it more memorable. Rhetorical triangles can be used to create a logical structure for your argument and make it more persuasive.

Finally, it's important to keep in mind that persuasion is not about manipulating or tricking people. It's about understanding the needs and desires of your audience and providing them with a solution that meets those needs. By understanding your audience and providing them with value, you can create persuasive copy that is both ethical and effective.

In summary, many different persuasion techniques can be used in copywriting, and understanding and applying them effectively can make a significant difference in the effectiveness of your copy. From social proof, authority, scarcity, reciprocity, emotional appeals, storytelling, and rhetorical devices, to understanding your audience and providing value, these techniques can all be used to create a persuasive and effective copy on Fiverr. By applying these techniques to your own copywriting, you'll be able to create persuasive and effective copy that drives results and boost your Fiverr sales.

The Role of Storytelling in Persuasion

In this section of the book, we will be discussing the role of storytelling in persuasion. Storytelling is a powerful tool that can be used to capture attention, build emotional connections, and drive action. By crafting compelling stories that align with your message, you can use them to persuade your audience.

Humans have been telling stories for thousands of years, and it's no surprise that storytelling is such an effective persuasion technique. Storytelling allows us to connect with our audience on an emotional level, and create a sense of empathy and understanding. When a story is well-crafted, it can make the audience feel as though they are a part of the story, and that they are experiencing the same emotions as the characters.

One way storytelling can be used in copywriting is by highlighting the problem that a product or service solves. By telling a story about how a product or service helped a customer overcome a particular problem, you can create a sense of empathy with the audience, and make it more likely that they will take action. For example, if you are selling a weight loss program on Fiverr, telling the story of how the program helped someone lose weight and improve their health can be more effective than just listing the features of the program.

Another way storytelling can be used in copywriting is by highlighting the benefits of a product or service. By telling a story about how a product or service improved someone's life, you can create a sense of excitement and anticipation with the audience, and make it more likely that they will take action. For example, if you are selling a guitar lesson on Fiverr, telling the story of how the lessons helped someone become a great guitar player can be more effective than just listing the features of the lesson.

Finally, storytelling can also be used to create a sense of urgency. By telling a story about how a product or service is only available for a limited time, you can create a sense of urgency with the audience, and make it more likely that they will take action. For example, if you are selling a service on Fiverr that is only available for a limited time, telling a story about how the service helped someone achieve their goal can create a sense of urgency and make it more likely that someone will buy the service.

In conclusion, storytelling is a powerful tool that can be used to capture attention, build emotional connections, and drive action. By crafting compelling stories that align with your message, you can use them to persuade your audience on Fiverr. By understanding the role of storytelling in persuasion, you'll be able to create persuasive and effective copy that drives results and boost your Fiverr sales.

CRAFTING A COMPELLING COPY

How to write headlines that grab attention

In this section of the book, we will focus on how to write headlines that grab attention and make your copy more effective. A headline is the first thing that people will see when they come across your copy, and it must be attention-grabbing and compelling. A great headline can make the difference between someone reading your copy and moving on to the next thing.

First, let's talk about the importance of headlines. Headlines are important because they are the first thing that people will see when they come across your copy. They are responsible for capturing attention and making people want to read more. A great headline can make the difference between someone reading your copy and moving on to the next thing.

Next, let's talk about how to write headlines that grab attention. The most important thing to keep in mind when writing headlines is that they should be attention-grabbing and compelling. Here are a few tips to help you write headlines that grab attention:

i. **Keep it short and sweet:** Headlines should be short and to the point. They should be easy to read and understand.

ii. **Use power words:** Power words are words that are emotional and evocative. They can be used to create a sense of urgency or excitement. Examples of power words include "amazing," "proven," "revolutionary," "breakthrough," etc.

iii. **Ask a question:** Asking a question in a headline can be a great way to grab attention. It makes people curious and encourages them to read more.

iv. **Use numbers:** Numbers are attention-grabbing and can be used to create a sense of urgency. For example, "5 Proven Ways to Boost Your Fiverr Sales" is more attention-grabbing than "Ways to Boost Your Fiverr Sales"

v. **Use action words:** Action words are words that encourage the reader to take action. Examples of action words include "discover," "unlock," "reveal," etc.

In addition to these tips, it's also important to keep in mind that headlines should be relevant and align with the rest of the copy. The headline should reflect the content of the copy and be an accurate representation of what the reader can expect to find.

In conclusion, headlines are crucial for capturing attention and making your copy more effective. By keeping headlines short and sweet, using powerful words, asking questions, using numbers and action words, and aligning with the rest of the copy, you can create headlines that grab attention and make your copy more effective on Fiverr. By following these tips, you'll be able to create headlines that grab attention and drive results, boosting your Fiverr sales.

The Art of Crafting Persuasive Body Copy

In this section of the book, we will focus on how to craft persuasive body copy that drives results. Persuasive body copy is the main content of your copywriting, and it must be compelling and persuasive. A great body copy can make the difference between someone taking action or moving on to the next thing.

First, let's talk about the importance of body copy. Body copy is important because it's the main content of your copywriting, and it's responsible for providing the information that people need to make a decision. A great body copy can make the difference between someone taking action or moving on to the next thing.

Next, let's talk about how to craft persuasive body copy. The most important thing to keep in mind when crafting body copy is that it should be persuasive and compelling. Here are a few tips to help you craft persuasive body copy:

i. **Use persuasive language:** Persuasive language is a language that is designed to influence and persuade. Examples of persuasive language include "you," "proven," "guaranteed," "limited time," etc.

ii. **Use statistics and data:** Statistics and data are persuasive because they provide evidence to back up your claims. Use statistics and data to provide evidence of the effectiveness of your product or service.

iii. **Use testimonials:** Testimonials are persuasive because they provide social proof. Use testimonials from satisfied customers to show that your product or service is effective.

iv. **Use storytelling:** Storytelling is persuasive because it allows you to connect with your audience on an emotional level. Use storytelling to create a sense of empathy and understanding with your audience.

v. **Use a call to action:** A call to action is a persuasive technique that encourages the reader to take action. Use a clear and compelling call to action at the end of your body copy to encourage the reader to take action, such as "Buy now" or "Sign up today".

vi. **Use formatting:** Use formatting techniques such as bullet points, headings, and subheadings to make your copy easy to read and skim. This makes it more likely that people will read through your entire message and take action.

vii. **Use clear and simple language:** Make sure your language is clear and simple, avoiding industry jargon or complex terms that can make it harder for readers to understand and engage with your message.

It's also important to keep in mind that your body copy should align with your headline and overall message. The body copy should provide more information and details about the product or service, but it should also support and reinforce the message conveyed in the headline.

In conclusion, crafting persuasive body copy is crucial for driving results. By using persuasive language, statistics and data, testimonials, storytelling, a clear call to action, formatting, and clear and simple language, you can create body copy that is compelling and persuasive. By following these tips, you'll be able to create a persuasive body copy that drives results and boost your Fiverr sales. Remember to align your body copy with your headline and overall message to make sure it supports and reinforces the message you're trying to convey.

How to use language to influence and persuade

In this section of the book, we will focus on how to optimize your copy for the Fiverr platform. Optimizing your copy for

Fiverr means tailoring it to the specific requirements and characteristics of the platform, to make it as effective as possible.

First, it's important to understand the audience and what they are looking for on Fiverr. Fiverr is a marketplace where people go to find freelancers and services for various tasks. This means that your copy should be focused on highlighting the value and benefits of your service or gig, and how it can help the customer achieve their goal.

Next, it's important to use the features of the Fiverr platform to your advantage. This includes using keywords in your gig title and description, adding images and videos to showcase your service, and highlighting any relevant certifications or qualifications you may have. Additionally, you can use Fiverr's review and rating system to showcase positive feedback from previous customers to increase the perceived value of your service.

It's also important to keep in mind the competition on Fiverr. There are thousands of other freelancers and service providers on the platform, so it's important to make sure your copy stands out. This can be achieved by using persuasive language and highlighting unique selling points of your service that sets you apart from others.

In addition, make sure to use a clear and compelling call to action in your gig description, encouraging the customer to take action and purchase your service. Make it easy for them to understand the next step they need to take to work with you.

By understanding your audience, using the features of the platform, highlighting unique selling points, and using a clear call to action, you can make your copy stand out from the competition and increase your chances of success. Additionally, it's important to be consistent with your branding, use images, videos and other visual elements to showcase your service and make sure to keep your gig and profile updated with the most recent information and feedback. By following these tips, you'll be able to optimize your copy for the Fiverr platform and increase your chances of success on the platform. Remember to keep testing and experimenting with different strategies to see what works best for you and your target audience on Fiverr.

Another important aspect of optimizing your copy for Fiverr is to understand the structure and layout of the platform. This includes understanding how gigs are organized and displayed, and how customers navigate through the platform. For example, it's important to use relevant tags and categories for your gig to ensure that it appears in the correct search results. Additionally, it's important to use a clear and consistent layout for your gig description, making it easy for customers to find the information they need.

Furthermore, it's crucial to keep in mind the character limit and formatting requirements of Fiverr. Make sure your gig title and description are within the character limit and utilize formatting options such as bullet points and headings to make your copy easy to read and skim. This will ensure that your gig stands out and is more likely to be clicked on.

Lastly, it's important to stay up-to-date with the latest trends, best practices and changes on the Fiverr platform. Fiverr is constantly evolving and updating its features, so it's important to stay informed and adapt your copy accordingly. This will help you stay ahead of the competition and ensure that your copy is optimized for the platform.

In summary, optimizing your copy for Fiverr is crucial for increasing your chances of success on the platform. By understanding the audience, using the features of the platform, highlighting unique selling points, and using a clear call to action, understanding the structure and layout of the platform, staying within the character limit, formatting requirements and staying up-to-date with the latest trends, you can make your copy stand out and increase your chances of success.

OPTIMIZING FOR FIVERR

Strategies for Creating Effective Fiverr Gig Descriptions

Creating an effective Fiverr gig description is crucial for attracting potential buyers and increasing your chances of making a sale. A well-crafted gig description can help to showcase your skills, highlight your experience, and set your gig apart from the competition. Here are some strategies for creating effective Fiverr gig descriptions:

i. **Use a clear and compelling headline:** Your headline is the first thing potential buyers will see when they come across your gig. Make sure it is clear, compelling, and accurately describes the services you are offering.

ii. **Highlight your unique selling points:** Use your gig description to showcase your unique selling points and what sets you apart from other sellers. This could be your experience, qualifications, or unique approach to the services you are offering.

iii. **Use keywords:** Use keywords in your gig description that are relevant to the services you are offering. This will help to increase the visibility of your gig in search results.

iv. **Use images and videos:** Use images and videos in your gig description to showcase your work and give potential buyers a better idea of what to expect. This can help to increase engagement and make your gig stand out from the competition.

v. **Include testimonials:** Including testimonials from past clients can help to build trust and credibility with potential buyers. Make sure to include testimonials that are specific and relevant to the services you are offering.

vi. **Be specific:** Make sure to be specific about the services you are offering, the deliverables, and the timeframe. This will help to avoid confusion and increase the chances of making a sale.

vii. **Provide a clear call to action:** End your gig description with a clear call to action that tells potential buyers what they should do next. This could be to place an order, ask a question or request a custom quote.

viii. **Review and Revise:** Review your gig description regularly and make revisions as needed. This will help to ensure that it is up-to-date and reflective of the services you are currently offering.

By following these strategies, you can create an effective gig description that will help to attract potential buyers and increase your chances of making a sale on Fiverr. Remember to keep your gig description concise, clear, and easy to understand, and to use images, videos and testimonials to showcase your work and build trust with potential buyers. By regularly reviewing and updating your gig description, you can ensure that it is always up-to-date and reflective of the services you are offering.

Tips for using Fiverr's platform to your advantage:

Fiverr is a powerful platform that can help you to reach new customers and grow your business. Here are some tips for using Fiverr's platform to your advantage:

i. **Optimize your profile:** Make sure your profile is complete and includes a clear and professional profile picture, a detailed bio, and a list of your skills and experience. This will help to increase your visibility on the platform and make it easier for potential buyers to find you.

ii. **Use keywords:** Use relevant keywords in your gig titles, descriptions, and tags to increase your visibility in search results. This will make it easier for potential buyers to find your gigs when searching for specific services.

iii. **Create detailed gig descriptions:** Make sure your gig descriptions are detailed, clear, and easy to understand. This will help potential buyers to understand the services you are offering and make it more likely that they will place an order.

iv. **Use images and videos:** Use images and videos in your gig descriptions to showcase your work and give potential buyers a better idea of what to expect. This can help to increase engagement and make your gigs stand out from the competition.

v. Respond to buyer requests: Make sure to respond to buyer requests promptly and provide detailed information about the services you are offering. This will help to build trust and credibility with potential buyers.

vi. **Get positive reviews:** Encourage your customers to leave positive reviews for your gigs. Positive reviews can help to increase your visibility on the platform and make it more likely that potential buyers will place an order.

vii. **Use Fiverr's analytics tools:** Use Fiverr's analytics tools to track your gig's performance and identify areas for improvement. This will help you to optimize your gigs and improve your visibility on the platform.

By following these tips, you can use Fiverr's platform to your advantage and reach new customers

How to Use Customer Feedback to Improve Copywriting

Customer feedback is an important tool for improving your copywriting on Fiverr. By paying attention to what your customers have to say, you can identify areas for improvement and make changes that will help to increase conversions and revenue. Here are some tips for using customer feedback to improve your copywriting:

i. **Pay attention to what your customers are saying:** Read your customer reviews and pay attention to the feedback they are giving you. Look for patterns in the feedback and identify areas where you can improve.

ii. **Use feedback to improve your headlines:** Use customer feedback to identify which headlines are working well and which ones aren't. This will help you to create more effective headlines that will help to increase engagement and conversions.

iii. **Use feedback to improve your calls-to-action:** Use customer feedback to identify which calls-to-action are working well and which ones aren't. This will help you to create more effective calls-to-action that will help to increase conversions.

iv. **Use feedback to improve your images and videos:** Use customer feedback to identify which images and videos are working well and which ones aren't. This will help you to create more effective images and videos that will help to increase engagement and conversions.

v. **Use feedback to improve your overall message:** Use customer feedback to identify which messages are resonating with your target audience and which ones aren't. This will help you to create more effective messages that will help to increase conversions.

By paying attention to customer feedback, you can identify areas for improvement and make changes that will help to increase conversions and revenue. Remember that using feedback to improve your copywriting is an ongoing process and that you should continue to gather feedback and make changes as necessary.

MEASURING SUCCESS FOR FIVERR

Setting measurable goals

As a Fiverr seller, it is important to understand the impact of your persuasive copywriting on your clients' businesses. One of the most effective ways to do this is by setting measurable goals. This helps you to understand how your copy is resonating with your clients' target audience and achieving the desired outcome.

When setting goals, it is important to consider the specific needs of your clients. For example, if a client is looking to increase website traffic, a specific goal for your copywriting would be "increase website traffic by 25% in the next three months." This gives you a clear target to work towards and a timeline to measure progress.

Another important aspect of setting goals is to ensure they align with your clients' overall business objectives. For example, if your client's main goal is to generate leads, then your copywriting goal should be focused on driving conversions, such as "increase conversions on the contact form by 50% in the next two months."

Once you have set your goals, it's important to communicate them clearly to your clients and track your progress. This will help you to continually improve your copywriting efforts and achieve better results over time.

Analyzing data and metrics

In order to measure the success of your copywriting efforts, it is essential to track the right metrics. This includes website traffic, conversions, bounce rate, time on site, and engagement metrics such as likes, shares and comments.

You should also use tools such as Google Analytics, heat mapping, and A/B testing to gain insight into user behavior and how they interact with your clients' website. For example, heat mapping can show you which elements of the website are drawing the most attention, while A/B testing can help you identify which version of your copy is more effective.

By analyzing data and metrics, you can gain a better understanding of what is working and what isn't. This information can then be shared with your clients to show them the impact of your copywriting efforts and help them to make informed decisions about their website.

Continuously testing and improving copy

Measuring success is not a one-time event, but rather an ongoing process. It is important to continuously test and improve your copy in order to achieve the best results. This means not only monitoring metrics, but also making adjustments based on the data you collect.

For example, if you notice that website traffic has increased but conversions have not, this may indicate that your copy is not effectively persuading visitors to take action. In this case, you should consider testing different calls-to-action or adjusting the structure of your copy to make it more persuasive.

Continuous testing and improvement also means staying up-to-date with the latest trends and best practices in persuasive copywriting. This could include attending industry events, reading relevant blogs and publications, and taking courses to improve your skills.

As a Fiverr seller, it is important to be transparent with your clients about your testing and improvement process. This will help them to understand the impact of your work and give them the confidence to continue working with you in the future.

In conclusion, measuring the success of persuasive copywriting is essential for achieving the desired outcome for your clients' businesses. By setting measurable goals, analyzing data and metrics, and continuously testing and improving your copy, you can ensure that your efforts are having the desired impact and achieving your clients' business objectives. This will not only help you to retain your clients but also attract new clients, as your clients will be able to see the value of your service.

CONCLUSION

Recap of the Key Takeaways from the Book

In this book, we have covered various techniques and strategies that can be used to make copywriting more persuasive and successful on Fiverr.

We discussed the importance of crafting a compelling headline, and how to use formatting, action words, numbers, and questions to make headlines more attention-grabbing and align with the overall message.

We also looked at the importance of using subheadings effectively in copywriting. By using descriptive and informative subheadings, formatting, keywords, parallel structure, and keeping them short, you can use subheadings to make your copy more persuasive and successful on Fiverr.

In addition, we highlighted the importance of calls to action in copywriting. By being clear and specific, using action words, creating a sense of urgency, making it prominent and testing and iterating to improve results, you can use calls to action effectively to drive results and boost your Fiverr sales.

We also discussed how to use testimonials effectively in copywriting. By using real testimonials, quotes, images, and a variety of testimonials, and placing them in a prominent location, you can make your copy more persuasive and successful on Fiverr.

Lastly, we talked about the importance of storytelling in copywriting. By using relatable characters, conflict and resolution, descriptive language and aligning with your message, you can use storytelling to create a connection with your audience and convey your message in a way that is both memorable and relatable.

In addition to the techniques mentioned above, the book also discussed the importance of research and understanding your target audience. By researching your target audience, you can gain insight into their needs, pain points, and preferences. This will help you to craft copy that speaks directly to them and addresses their specific needs. Understanding your target audience will also help you to choose the right tone, language and imagery to use in your copy.

Another key takeaway from the book is the importance of proofreading and editing your copy. This will help to ensure that your copy is free of errors and is easy to read and understand. It will also help to ensure that your message is communicated clearly and effectively.

It also emphasized the use of storytelling, which can be a powerful tool for engaging the reader and making your copy more persuasive and successful. By using relatable characters, conflict and resolution, descriptive language, and aligning with your message, you can use storytelling to create a connection with your audience and convey your message in a way that is both memorable and relatable.

Lastly, the book also emphasized the importance of testing and iterating your copy. This will help you to determine what works and what doesn't and will allow you to make improvements and optimize your copy over time, by using these techniques, you can create copy that is more persuasive and successful on Fiverr, which can help increase conversions and revenue. Remember to stay true to your message and overall tone, and to constantly test and iterate to improve results.

In conclusion, the key takeaways from this book include the importance of crafting a compelling headline, using subheadings effectively, using calls to action, using testimonials, understanding your target audience, proofreading and editing your copy, using storytelling, and testing and iterating your copy. By implementing these techniques, you can create copy that is more persuasive and successful on Fiverr, and help increase conversions and revenue.

Encouragement to Put the Book's Teachings into Action

Writing copy can be challenging, but by implementing the techniques discussed in this book, you can make your copy more persuasive and successful on Fiverr. Remember that the key to success is to stay true to your message and overall tone, and to constantly test and iterate to improve results.

It's important to not get discouraged if your first attempts at writing copy don't lead to immediate results. Keep in mind that crafting effective copy takes time and practice. Take the time to research your target audience, and use the techniques discussed in the book to craft compelling headlines, subheadings, calls to action, and more.

Don't be afraid to experiment and try new things. Test different headlines, subheadings, and calls to action to see what works best for your target audience. Remember that testing and iterating your copy is an ongoing process and that even small changes can lead to big results.

Also, don't forget to proofread and edit your copy to ensure that it is free of errors and is easy to read and understand. This will help to ensure that your message is communicated clearly and effectively.

In summary, the key is to take action and put the book's teachings into practice. With time and practice, you will be able to create copy that is more persuasive and successful on Fiverr. Keep in mind that the process of crafting effective copy is ongoing and that testing and iterating your copy is essential to achieving success. So, don't be afraid to experiment and try new things, and keep working at it. You'll be surprised at the results you can achieve.

Additional Resources for Further Learning and Improvement

There are many additional resources available for further learning and improvement in copywriting. Here are a few examples:

Copywriting books - There are many books available on the subject of copywriting, covering topics such as headlines, subheadings, calls to action, and more. Some popular books include "Influence: The Psychology of Persuasion" by Robert Cialdini, "Made to Stick" by Chip Heath and Dan Heath, and "Contagious: How to Build Word of Mouth in the Digital Age" by Jonah Berger.

Copywriting courses - There are many online courses available on the subject of copywriting, covering topics such as headlines, subheadings, calls to action, and more. Some popular courses include "Copywriting Mastery" by Neil Patel, "Copywriting Secrets" by Jim Edwards, and "Copywriting Academy" by Ray Edwards.

Copywriting blogs - There are many blogs available that cover the subject of copywriting, providing tips, tricks, and strategies for writing persuasive copy. Some popular blogs include Copyblogger, Airstory, and Men with Pens.

Copywriting communities - There are many online communities of copywriters that you can join to share ideas, ask questions and get feedback on your work. Some popular communities include CopyHackers, Copywriting community, and Copywriters' Cafe.

Copywriting podcasts - There are many podcasts available that cover the subject of copywriting, providing tips, tricks, and strategies for writing persuasive copy. Some popular podcasts include Copyblogger FM, The Copywriter Club and Copywriting Marketing.

By studying these resources, you will be able to improve your understanding of copywriting and pick up new tips, tricks, and strategies to improve your writing. Remember to practice what you learn and test your copy to see what works best for your target audience. With time and practice, you will become a skilled copywriter and achieve success on Fiverr.

ENDNOTE

In conclusion, this book has provided a comprehensive guide on how to make your copywriting more persuasive and successful on Fiverr. We have discussed the importance of crafting a compelling headline, using subheadings effectively, using calls to action, using testimonials, understanding your target audience, proofreading and editing your copy, using storytelling, and testing and iterating your copy. We also discussed the importance of research and understanding your target audience, and encouraged taking action and putting the book's teachings into practice. We also provided additional resources for further learning and improvement in copywriting. Remember that the key to success is to stay true to your message and overall tone, and to constantly test and iterate to improve results. With time and practice, you will be able to create copy that is more persuasive and successful on Fiverr and achieve success on the platform.

It's also important to remember that copywriting is an ongoing process, and that there is always room for improvement. Keeping up with the latest trends and techniques in copywriting is essential for continued success. The internet is a great resource for keeping yourself updated with the latest tips, tricks and strategies in copywriting.

Furthermore, it's important to keep in mind that copywriting is not just about selling a product or service, it's also about building relationships with your audience. By understanding your audience and speaking to them in a relatable, authentic way, you can build trust and credibility with them. This will help you to create long-term customer relationships and drive conversions and sales on Fiverr.

In the end, the key to success in copywriting is to be willing to put in the time and effort. It takes practice, patience, and persistence to become a skilled copywriter. So, be persistent and keep working at it, you'll be surprised at the results you can achieve.

This book has been designed to be a guide for new and experienced copywriters, and I hope you have found it informative and useful. I wish you all the best in your copywriting journey and success on Fiverr.